T0142419

Life with the Sioux People in times gone by

As told by Blue Feather to Claire Loryman

CLAIRE LORYMAN

© 2022 Claire Loryman. All rights reserved.

Blue Feather Painting is copyrighted by Patrick Gamble.

No part of this book may be reproduced, stored in a retrieval system, or transmitted by any means without the written permission of the author.

AuthorHouse™ UK
1663 Liberty Drive
Bloomington, IN 47403 USA
www.authorhouse.co.uk
UK TFN: 0800 0148641 (Toll Free inside the UK)
UK Local: 02036 956322 (+44 20 3695 6322 from outside the UK)

Because of the dynamic nature of the Internet, any web addresses or links contained in this book may have changed since publication and may no longer be valid. The views expressed in this work are solely those of the author and do not necessarily reflect the views of the publisher, and the publisher hereby disclaims any responsibility for them.

Any people depicted in stock imagery provided by Getty Images are models, and such images are being used for illustrative purposes only. Certain stock imagery © Getty Images.

This book is printed on acid-free paper.

ISBN: 978-1-6655-9675-6 (sc)
ISBN: 978-1-6655-9674-9 (e)

Print information available on the last page.

Published by AuthorHouse 03/02/2022

authorHOUSE®

Introduction

Blue Feather was a Sioux Wiseman who is very eager to tell his story. He and his tribe lived in North Dakota, many, many moons ago. It was a time of great change. European settlers were forging their way across "their" land. He becomes very angry about these people, with "their greed and their guns" He thinks there is room for them all; enough land to share. His emotion is evident in his poetry. He himself never had a gun, only a bow and a quiver of arrows and he was an expert horseman. If you look carefully at his portrait you will note that the feather hanging from Blue Feather's hair is not all blue. This denotes the fact that he was killed (shot?) before middle age.

The portrait of Blue Feather is painted by Patrick Gamble, a now well known artist who lives in Cornwall. The other beautiful paintings, inspired by Blue Feather's story, are done by Kate Roberts. Kate was a bit hesitant to embark on the project, but Blue Feather knew she would do well. Thank you to both of you for enhancing his story.

I have known of Blue Feather from my early teens. My parents, together with three friends had a meditation group. To further their understanding they visited the famous medium, Estelle Roberts, whose Guide was Red Cloud. This was in the 1950s' My father was introduced to Blue Feather, and from then on I was referred to as "the Papoose" Many years later, after my Father had passed to Spirit, Blue Feather started communicating with me. This collection of poetry is the result. While I was writing it down it was all so vivid! I could see and hear the wind roaring, the icicles tinkling. I could both hear and see the small animals scampering in the leaves in the winter. I have been a wolf treading through the packed snow in mid winter, with his attention drawn to a rustling in the bare bushes nearby. I briefly wondered why my paws weren't cold on the ice! The cold, silence of the night time gazing up at the canopy of stars, being alone in the quiet?

I especially find "Falling leaves" interesting, "tales of many moons" and "carry on the legends and the wisdom." "Wisdom not written, remembered for the future"

Once I was flying down across the mid states to California, possibly across the Dakotas' I was being prompted to find pen and paper! "The bird glides down" was the result! The last poem "Why, Why Worry" appeared much later, but I decided to include it.

Recently I introduced Blue Feather's poetry to some friends and they could see Blue Feather standing behind me!

When I visited Kate's house for a delicious lunch with a couple of friends, Kate and I were to talk about her illustrating Blue Feather's poems. I decided I needed a post prandial nap after such a good meal. I took myself into another room but quickly realised Blue Feather wanted to talk to Kate.

So, I fetched her and we sat down. Blue Feather was close enough to me to talk to Kate. Afterwards she told me it was not me talking but Blue Feather.

Concise Sioux history

The Colonial frontier moved westward in the mid C19th and also the California gold rush in 1849 opened a floodgate of prospectors. Many Sioux became incensed by the US government's attempts to establish the Bozeman Trail and other routes through the Tribe's sovereign lands. The US sought to forestall strife by negotiating the 1st Treaty of Fort Laramie (1851) with the Sioux and other Plains people. The treaty assigned territories to each tribe throughout the northern Great Plains. 1865-67 the Oglala Chief, Red Cloud, led thousands of Sioux warriors in a campaign to halt construction of the Bozeman Trail. In 1868 the US government agreed to abandon the trail and guaranteed the Sioux people exclusive possession of the present state of South Dakota, west of the Missouri river. When gold was discovered in the Black hills of South Dakota in the mid 1870s thousands of miners disregarded the treaty and swarmed onto the Sioux reservation. There were years of unrest with great hardship for the Sioux. In 1890 was the battle at Wounded Knee Creek with the massacre of 200 Sioux men, women and children. After that the Sioux ceased military resistance.

Red Cloud (1822-1909) was one of the most important leaders of the Oglala Lakota from 1868 to 1909. He was one of the most capable Native American opponents whom the US army faced in the invasion of the Western Territories.

Claire Loryman

Contents

The World is Beautiful.

The hills stretch on forever, forever,
you walk on forever to reach the other side.
Time stretches on forever, forever.
The air is sweet, the flowers are beautiful.
The insects fly on their daily tasks.
The air is sweet, the world is still.
The cobwebs catch the Essence, the wonderful Essence.
To meditate in the open is to "open one's mind."
The land is at peace, the time is quiet.
The birds come, the snake appears, the earth is at peace, at peace.
One is aware of nature, it is the real world.
The world is true, we should be part of it.
Animals are innocent. We are part of the world.
Oh child, do not lose it! It is our connection,
to see the sun, to see the moon,
to see the trees with their winter branches.
Consider the winter sun, with all its beauty.
Be thankful for the rain as it gently falls.
The bears are around, they do not appear.
The mice scurry around, they make their nests.
They are part of nature, part of the universe.
The birds of prey, they are wise and watchful.
They are alert, always alert. They feed their young,
they are wise, they protect. The animals in the field,
they munch the grass, they are free.
Life is unadulterated, life as it should be.
The bear appears. The fox is watching for the next meal.
The sky is blue. The clouds come, they bring the rain
onto the grass. Grass is now green.

We are all part of the world. We should think.
We should meditate. We are part of nature.
We need each other. We are not alone.
We should be aware of each other.
We should help each other, support each other,
that is how the world should be.

Man destroys it, with his guns and his greed!
He is too greedy for land, never satisfied!
Never content! Why? They do not understand nature.
They are not part of the real world.
They turn on themselves, they look to each other.
They do not look outwards, they do not see what is around them.
They are not part of the real world.
They do not progress! They stagnate!

The world is beautiful! Consider the sun!
Consider the stars! Watch the cobwebs!
The bear is watching you! The fish are alert, they watch around.
The trees are beautiful, especially in the winter.
How beautiful the world, for us all to see, for us all to share.
There for us all, but we need to be aware.
The gift is gone with modern man, but he has eyes to see?
But chooses not to! Why? The world is there,
the beautiful world, with all its glory!
With cobwebs and insects, just reach out and touch!
Reach for the sun! Reach for the moon!
Just listen! Just stop and listen!
The world is beautiful, the world is at peace for us all.
So if we stop, if we listen……..
Reach for the sun, reach for the stars!
We are here in the real world.

Image copyright Kate Roberts

Winter landscape

The stream was cool, rushing along.
The stream was very blue,
rushing over the stones below,
the cool, cool waters of North Dakota.
Land of the free, to roam at will.
Now no longer free, no longer free,
with the beautiful sun, the beautiful stars,
the warm sun with the splendid sunsets,
with fiery glow. the promise of morning.
The dawn of day, the pale yellow sun.
A day of promise, with much to be done.
The rivers of light, through the trees,
the beautiful trees, their branches spreading.
The warmth of the sun, the warmth shedding,
shedding its warmth over all the land.

Praise be to God for the beautiful morning.
A brand new day, a day with promise.
A day for forgetting, forgiving the past.
A day for renewing, rejoicing and sharing.
Oh man! Can't you see? See what you are missing?
Each day as it dawns, is another day.
Another day to assess. a day that is new.
We all praise the Lord, both me and you.
Both me and you, and that **does** mean you.
A day for us all, we can all start anew.
We all should be looking, we all have the sense.
We all have our stumbles, but it all makes good sense.

The trees, they are sparkling, sparkling in the snow.
The branches, they tremble, with
the weight of the snow.
The snow, it is glistening in the winter sun.
The ice is reflected, in the pale winter sun.
The sky, it is azure with the beautiful morning.
The bear, he is watching, treading a path,
a path through the snow, treading warily.
He is leaving his footprints, which freeze in the snow.
The sun is reflected on the ice in the snow,
the flattened snow from the bear's paw prints.

The big, wide paw prints of the wonderful bear.
How dependable, how solid, how dependable the bear.
But unleash his strength, when it is needed.
His paws are massive, his claws are massive.
But meals are needed and families to feed.
Waters are cold, but a fish beneath will do,
will do for a meal, in a desperate attempt,
if nothing appears in the winter landscape.
But bears, they are beautiful, part of the scene.

Then walk in the snow, you see where he's been.
Oh! Think of the sun, think of the snow.
We all need the landscape, with the sun's glow.
Oh man! Won't you look? Won't you see
the beautiful world, for us all to see.
Reach for the sun. Reach for the moon.
Reach for the stars. Look at the moon.
All there for us all, why does man ignore?

The bear in the landscape, the bear on the hill,
the symbol of earth, so solid and round.
The beautiful fur, it glows in the sun.
To roll in the snow, with the snow on his fur,
his beautiful sleek fur, the wonderful cover,
so useful to man, when no longer needed.
The bear's claws, the huge bear claws; so strong.
A symbol of huge unleashed strength.
A strength to the wearer, the bearer of claws.
A symbol of strength, but that is his downfall,
for all becomes useful, all parts of the bear,
all items of clothing, they come from the bear.
Man traps, man kills, just that he may share
the beautiful fur, the beautiful bear,
that man may be warm, that man might be strong.
Oh! Beautiful bear, you are lost to the world.
Oh! Beautiful bear, you are not forgotten.
The bear is still watching, in our wonderful world.
The bear is still there, wonderfully bold.
Oh! Look to the sun, look to the moon,
the beautiful world, for us all to see.

3

Image copyright Kate Roberts

The Wolf

The wolf is special, he has an affinity with man.
Man has forgotten, but it is all true, all so true.
Reach for the sun, reach for the stars,
the canopy of heaven, the stars up above.
Rise, rise, up, up, up among the stars,
the stars in the wonderful blue sky,
for all man to see. The wolf wanders
in the star light, in the clear star light.
He treads carefully, across the horizon,
a shadow on the horizon, in the clear moonlight.
A quiet shadow, in the distance, on the horizon.
Most of the world is asleep, but the wolf is contemplating.
He daintily picks his way through the bushes and trees.
He walks warily, listening for the slightest sound,
a rustle in the bushes, a tremble in the branches above,
up in the trees, the trees in full leaf,
with the wind whispering through, the gentle wind.
The undergrowth crackles under the wolf's feet.
The world is at peace. The world is quiet, so quiet.
A mouse scurries through the undergrowth.
The wolf pauses, and wonders who is abroad.
His eyes penetrate the darkness, through the bushes.
The darkness begins to fade, there is a pale yellow light
on the horizon. Morning is approaching, dawn is approaching.
A new day is beginning, a new day is dawning.
A day for reflection, a day for beginning.
Each day is new, each day for new things.
The past is behind, the future unknown.
The deeds of today, the seeds of tomorrow.
All life has beginnings, today is the start.
How wonderful the wolf, treading life as it comes!

Remember the connection, Oh man! One with nature,
rapport with the wolf, so precious and still?
Adopt his outlook, view the world as it comes.
Share your knowledge, Oh wolf, with mankind, as before!
Oh man, you must look, must look as before!
Open your eyes, and see what is there.
Man, now with his guns and his greed for the land!
Man, cannot we share? There is plenty of land!

The land has much fruit, much fruit to be shared,
but man had to own it and drive us all out!
The "magic" of nature was totally lost!
He turned his back completely on what was there,
was there to see! Open your eyes, man!
You will see if you look!
The wonderful creatures, especially the wolf,
the wolf on the horizon, watching the world.

The wolf, as he treads through the bushes and trees,
the wolf, as he watches, peers through the trees.
The light, it is changing, from the stars up above.
A pale yellow light is appearing, the dawn has arrived!
A new day has arrived, with it's fresh breeze.
A new day for forgiving, a new day has dawned.

Image copyright Kate Roberts

Falling leaves

The leaves are falling, in the autumn sun,
falling onto the forest floor, onto the soft earth beneath.
Gently falling, floating, beautiful coloured leaves.
Gently, gently falling, onto the earth beneath.
The forest floor is full of life, all the insects and animals.
The leaves cushioning the ground beneath, giving shelter
to all small animals and insects below.
Using the leaves for warmth and shelter,
the beautiful leaves, such vibrant colours of orange and gold.
To give warmth to all creatures, when the snow begins to fall,
softly falling in the winter air. Softly, softly falling
from the sky above, down, down, down through the branches,
settling on the now bare branches of the trees,
and falling, falling onto the leaves beneath.
But all animals are safe in the leaves, leaves that rustle
as they scamper through, finding their winter stores.
Small animals with their burrows, their holes in the ground,
in the hollow of the roots of the trees, where there are gaps
for small homes, safe and secure, with the leaves for warmth,
and the companionship of others.

Man needs companionship, cannot survive alone,
but moves away from the simple way of life.
Time for chatter, for talking, for telling tales.
Time to assess the past year, look back on the year,
with the past seasons, the hunting, the companionship.
Of tales of many, many years from the Wise ones!
Tales told from father to son, from many moons,
many stories from many, many moons.
Winter is time to consider, time to tell the new ones
of all the old ways, of many, many stories.
Listen, my child, and you will learn from the Wise ones,
but you must sit and ponder, sit and listen, consider.
Really absorb and sit quietly, consider the words of the Wise ones,
of tales of many moons, wisdom from many moons,
from father to son. Carry on the legends and wisdom.
Wisdom, not written, but remembered, remembered for the future!
Wisdom, from the Wise ones. Sit and listen, take time to listen.
Sit in the quiet of the winter sun, the winter stars, and listen.
Gather round and listen to the Wise ones.

The winter leaves have fallen, the winter branches are bare.
The snow is lying on the ground beneath.
The small animals and insects are underneath in the leaves.
The larger animals are treading the snow above,
making interesting tracks, interweaving in the snow,
leaving the footprints in the snow, for all to see.
The winter sun sheds it's warmth over all the world.
The beautiful sun, to bring hope for the spring to come,
when the snows begin to melt, and the streams to fill,
to fill, and run into the rivers. The rivers with the rushing,
cold waters, cold from the winter snows.
The cold air, the frosty air, with the steam from man's breathing.
Cold crisp air, cold, cold, crisp, but the pale yellow sun,
the beautiful sun, spreads its pale light over the landscape.
The beautiful winter scene, the promise of spring to come.

Image copyright Kate Roberts

The end of winter

The sun shines on the frosty ground, the beautiful sun,
the sun of the morning, the sun of springtime,
the morning hastening, as the sun rises.
The earth, it is cold, frosty cold, cold in the morning.
The snows, they are gone, lost as the sun rises,
rises up in the sky, bringing spring's warmth,
warmth to arouse, awake all creatures from the winter time.
Time for renewing, restarting all things on the land.
A time so different from long ago, from many moons ago,
when it was the land of the free, the land of the free.
Now man with his guns, his greed for the land,
the land of our fathers, the land for the future,
but the future no more, the future no more.
We wish man would listen, would listen as before,
as before in times past, time before man
with his guns and his greed.
Time when all the land was free, free to wander
time when all animals roamed over the land.
The land of our fathers, from time immemorial,
time of the space, wide open spaces over all the land.
When man could roam, and animals were yonder
in the beautiful sun of the springtime to come,
when flowers will blossom and bloom.

Insects will fly and spiders weave their webs.
Insects will roam amongst the flowers, the beautiful flowers.
From the spring sun's rays, warming the land from the winter chill.
The spring sun that spreads the wonderful light,
which brings spring's warmth for us all to know.
The water rushes in the deep blue streams,
streams from the mountains, with the melted snows,
snow gone for the moment, but to return at the fall.
The trees spread their blossoms, their leaves to unfurl.
The land of the fathers, from time long ago,
many moons ago, from the stories of man,
wise men of the past, with the tales that were told
of history long gone. For life as it comes,
as the bumble bees pass, onwards, forever they go.

Life carries on from the seasons that pass,
the season that now arrives with the sun.
Oh man, look! Enjoy the life as it was.
Consider the past and what you have missed!
The ever changing seasons, the inevitable changes,
but always dependable, as the sun and the stars.
But man and his greed and his guns!
No more as life, the life of the past,
as long, long forgotten, changed for ever!
But why, oh why? Man is no happier now.
Man as he is, is ever changing the world,
never satisfied, never satisfied with things as they are.
So, look back in history, at things as they were,
as man lived with nature, much happier by far.

Summer morning

The summer sun shines over all the earth, all the earth,
with its warmth and beautiful light,
shedding warmth over all creation, over all the land.
The insects bask in the warmth, the spiders weave their webs,
their intricate webs. Gaze into their webs, their intricate webs,
with the morning dew glistening over the many threads.
As the sun shines through, casting shadows over the leaves
and branches, wavering in the soft breeze, as the sun rises,
rises high in the sky, the beautiful azure sky.
A beautiful morning, with the freshness, the start of a new day.
A day for forgiving, renewing, a new day to look forward.

Pause, man! Stop and look! Look at the spider's webs,
with the dew glistening, the webs juddering
and the dew drops twinkling in the sun's rays.
Winter has passed, spring has come, the sun is higher,
the sun is warmer, to warm the land.
All the animals are around, stirred into action with the new day.
The wolf has been abroad, before the sunrise, during the starlight,
when the stars were hanging in the sky, in the wide canopy of the sky,
the huge canopy of stars in the sky up above,
full of stars, twinkling their light over the land.
The moon casts the shadows in the starlight,
in the quiet world, the peaceful world.
The waters ripple in the cold streams, rattling over the pebbles below.
Even the fish are suspended in the water.
Even they are at peace, at peace with the world.
The world is so silent, except for the rustling of the wind
through the trees and bushes, shaking the newly made cobwebs
very gently, so gently. The spiders busy creating their webs
with never ending thread and energy.
The dew has not appeared yet, as it is still starlight.
The sun has yet to rise from the canopy of the stars,
has yet to spread its pale yellow light and warmth.
The dawn of a new day, new beginnings.
Man, pause and look, pause and ponder!
But man is too fast, too quick, too much to do,
doing so many things, finding more to do,
more to pack into his life, never satisfied, always striving,
striving for more, for better, for bigger! But stop! Pause!

Are you happy? Are you content? What do you gain?
Consider the sun, consider the stars!
Stop and listen, to the quiet world!
All is busy, but just the simple things in life.
Do you strive for the simple things, the basic things?
Are you happy? Are you content?
Stop and listen! Pause, stay awhile, sit and meditate.
Sit in the early morning light, while the world is quiet,
before the daily tasks, before the sun has risen high in the sky,
before the day's bustle has begun.
The sun sheds its warmth over all the land,
the beginning of another day to reflect and ponder,
a new day, a new beginning.

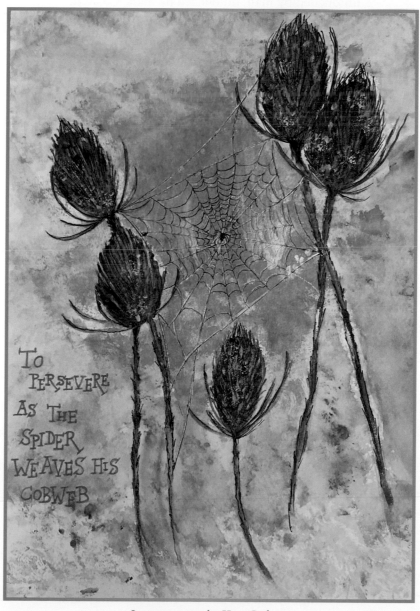

Image copyright Kate Roberts

By the shore of the lake

The shores of the lake are very blue, very blue.
Blue cool water, cool, deep water, with many fish,
many fish swimming around in the cool waters.
Cool waters to sit by, watching the reflections.
Watch the reflection of the sun and the moon,
the moon with the stars in the canopy up above,
the wonderful canopy up above, with the stars,
untouched by man, untouched by man. Created,
created by the WISE ONE, the wondrous Wise One,
the mysterious One who helped create all,
created the universe, the stars, the moon and the sun,
the blessed sun, which provides the gentle warmth,
the gentle warmth for us all to share, to share alike
for all creation, all birds and animals, the bear
and the fox, all insects and plants.
For all mankind, the gentle warmth, for all people.
The seasons, they pass, the sun and the moon,
each have their time, in the cycle of life.
The dependable cycle of all the seasons.
The rush of life for all mankind to share,
for each man to share, with no cost to each person.
The beautiful world is there, for us all to share,
to share in the harvest, to share in the harvest,
the harvest of nature, for all of mankind.
Plenty to share of nature's abundance,
but somehow man wants more, wants more,
wants better or different, is not satisfied.
But all of the harvest, all of earth's fruits
are there for us all, if only we share,
enough for us all, for us all to share!
But man had to be greedy with the land, the wide open spaces,
the land we could wander, could walk many valleys,
many valleys and plains, the grass and the meadows,
the fruits of the land, with the animals that wander,
the animals that wander with all of the seasons,
to follow the grassland, according to the seasons.
According to the seasons, with the sun and the moon,
the warmth of the sun and the cool refreshing rain,
the rain for the pastures, the streams and the rivers.
The rain falls on the pastures and plains,

water for man and water for animals,
water for insects and plants all alike.
The soft rain falling in the summer sun,
creating the colours, the beautiful rainbows,
the beautiful rainbows for all man to see.
The beautiful colours reflected in nature.
The colours reflected on the cool lake's waters,
the cool, cool waters, where the fish swim below.
To sit by the lake and look at the reflection,
the reflection above, of the sun and the moon,
the moon in the canopy, the canopy of the stars,
gone with the sun in the beautiful azure sky.

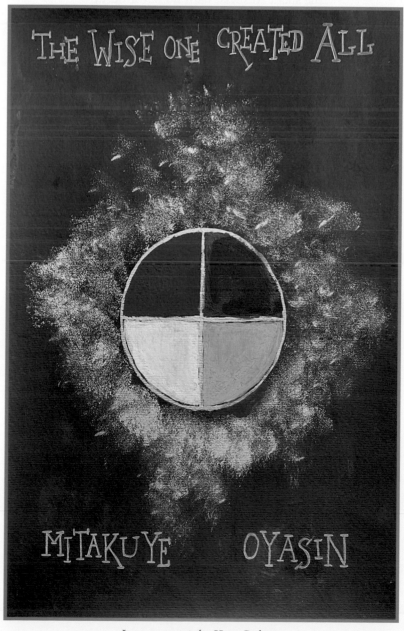

Image copyright Kate Roberts

The wonder of life

Silver beams from the moonlight, from the moonlight above,
striking through the branches of the trees, onto the ground below.
The earth is frosty cold, frost with the winter cold,
frost sparkling on the branches, on the bare winter branches.
So quiet, so quiet in the moonlight, in the pale moonlight,
so quiet, so silent. a stillness over the world,
the silent stillness, with no one around.
Birds are in shelter, in warmth, in the hedgerow.
The world is at peace, is at peace.
But low, the wolf is around, snuffling around,
seen in the moonlight, the pale frosty moonlight.
The stars up above, in the canopy of the sky,
the stars twinkling up above, twinkling in another world,
light reflected from the stars, lights up the world,
the wonderful world, the peaceful, peaceful world.

But no longer peaceful, with man and his guns!
Startled and disturbed, with life as it was,
interfered with the cycle of life, life as it was!
Gone now forever, changed completely forever,
lost forever, lost forever, changed forever!
All tales of the fathers, tales of many moons,
lost forever, now recalled, now remembered.
Listen my child, we will recapture some of the life,
life with its cycles, the rhythms of the seasons.
Life as it was, busy as it was, following the seasons,
following the cycle, the cycle of life.
Man does not look, does not pause, does not see,
does not see the canopy of stars, the stars and the moon,
shut in the world, locked in the world,
where none of them see the wonderful world, the wonderful world.
Does not live with nature, value nature, the cycle of the seasons,
never sits and ponders, never pauses to think.
The beauty of trees, the flowers and the hedgerows,
the basis of life, the value of friendship.
The companionship of sitting and viewing the world,
the sky with the sun, the moon and the stars.
Meditate, sit and ponder, sit and wonder.
Consider the creation, the wonderful creation!
The reason for life and how it all started,

how humble each man in the cycle of life,
to live through life in the natural world.
But man wanted space, wanted land in his plans,
his plans to expand on his ideas of wealth and greed!
But what value all this, did it give man wisdom?
It didn't bring happiness! Just drove us all out!
The land that we had, is ours no more!
Oh man, consider the stars, consider the moon,
watch the moonlight, the beams of the moonlight,
as it lights up trees, over the frosty cold ground.
The beautiful moonlight, as it lights up the world.

LISTEN MY CHILD,

WE WILL RECAPTURE

SOME OF THE LIFE...

LIFE AS IT WAS...

Image copyright Kate Roberts

Wisdom from the Wise One

The springtime, the blessed springtime, with the warming sun,
the warming sun, over all the land,
the land emerging from the winter cold,
the winter snows and frosts, the ice and the snow,
the icicles hanging from the branches of the bare winter trees,
now all melted and gone with the springtime sun.
The emerging world, as the sunshine spreads,
spreads across the landscape, awakening the trees and hedgerows
with the buds emerging and bursting, bursting their buds
into flowers and leaves, into flowers and leaves.
The wonderful flowers with the spectrum of colours,
mirrors the colours in the shades of the rainbow.
The rainbow as it appears, with the springtime rain
as it softly falls over all of the land,
the land, it flourishes and blossoms
with the gentle warmth of the springtime sun,
the wonderful warmth with the emerging world.
The animals, they wander in the sunshine,
bringing new life to all the world.
The time to consider the wonder of nature, the wonder of nature,
created by the WISE ONE, so long ago, so many moons ago.
The wonder of nature, considered by the Wiseman,
the Wiseman, who continues the traditions, the old ways of life.
Now no more, no more, when men came with their guns.
They came onto our land, across our land.
They wanted it all, to farm and to live, to fish and to hunt,
not share it with us, we had lived there so long,
so long, before time, before recent time of memories.
To live with the land, the sun and the moon,
together, with the stars, the stars up above,
the time of the seasons, the rhythm of life.

The time of the springtime, with the emerging warmth,
the time when the world emerges from the winter gloom.
Not all winter gloom, with the pale yellow sun,
the pale yellow sun shining over the frosty land.
The time past of cold days, of cold nights, long nights,
but we had the companionship, the companionship of each other.
Time for the tales and the stories of old, from time immemorial.
Times long past, when the WISE ONE created the world,
the world now bursting with life, with new life,
with life now awakening, with the sun of the springtime.
The blessed warmth spreading in a new spring day.
A time for considering the meaning of life,
the emergence of spring, in the cycle of life.

Image copyright Kate Roberts

The night sky

The moon in North Dakota is very bright, bright
in the clear beautiful azure sky, in the canopy of the stars.
The moon moves across in various waves,
as it dodges amongst the sky full of stars,
stars that have patterns, and their own destiny,
a destiny fulfilled as it crosses the sky.
Stars interweaving and moving in their various patterns.
Some in a design and some sit alone,
alone and brilliant, the light shimmers,
shimmers in the sky, as it weaves its own pattern,
dodging here and there, and crisscrossing along.
Some brilliant stars, which stand all alone
often appear for a while then seem to move away,
but others are there in their unique formations,
unique formations which dance in the sky.
One or two seem to stay where they are,
just occasionally move, then swing round as before.
The WISE ONE, who created, created the stars,
threw them into the sky, and there they have stayed,
stayed in the patterns, the patterns forever,
forever, immemorial, swinging around in the sky,
around in the sky, interweaving with the moon,
shines down on the earth, just shining and twinkling,
with various colours, they sparkle in the sky,
in the sky up above, in the canopy of the stars,
untouched by man, untouched by man.
Thrown there by the WISE ONE, the WISE ONE of all,
all of creation, from the beginning of life,
the creation of life, of many, many moons.
The stars, they are ancient, for all man to see,
to sit and ponder, wonder at the story of life,
not reached by man, never reached by man.
We live under the stars, in the land that we love,
the land that we share, in the land that we love,
the land we all share, with the cycle of nature.
The stars we all share, as the WISE ONE created.
But the land we have lost, we share it no more,
for man and his greed, with his guns
wanted the land and pushed us all out!
But we still have the stars and the moon up above

that the WISE ONE created, for all man to share.
Untouched by man, so safe for us all, to all gaze upon,
to ponder the creation, and all that it means.
The beautiful sky, the azure sky of the land where we lived,
the canopy of stars, with the moon up above.
The moon up above, for us all to share.
The pale moonlight, as it spreads over the land,
with the twinkling stars, on their pattern of life,
for us all to share, for us all to see,
to ponder the creation, and the destiny of man.

Image copyright Kate Roberts

The Lake

The shore of the lake, where the waters shake,
shakes the reeds along the edge, along the edge,
with the insects flying around and
spreading their wings,
their wings, to fly up and over the plants
and the reeds. The plants with their flowers opening
in the warm spring sunshine, opening their flowers
from the buds, from the buds, as they grow
in the warm sunshine and the rain, the gentle rain.
The gentle rain falls onto the flowers
and trickles down the leaves and the stems,
and tinkles into the water below, the cool water
of the lake, the still water, the still water
which reflects the spring sun, and
the plants on the edge,
the edge of the lake, with the plants and the insects.
The fish are beneath, suspended in the cool water,
then dart and dive around, looking for food,
for food and insects, that skate on the top,
the insects that balance on the water,
and fly up above, through and around the plants,
the plants that surround and grow on the edge.
The birds, they arrive, arrive from the north,
with the winter sunshine. They chase the insects,
the insects that live on the water and hidden, hidden
amongst the reeds on the edge of the lake.
The birds, they wade in the shallow water,
building their nests in the mudflats nearby.
Hiding places, in the shadow of the reeds,
protected under the reeds, the shelter of the reeds,
the shelter and shadows that protect
them from intruders.
But the young ones, the young ones, when they arrive,
they twitter and twatter, and give it away,

give it away, the place where they are hidden,
the place that was safe, but near animals are alerted,
alerted to the idea that there could be a meal.
The water, it splashes, as other animals arrive.
The men, they come fishing, to look for a meal.
The fish, they are caught by small fish suspended,
suspended, on end of a stick, which
stretches, stretches out
from man's hand, to reach in the water, the cool water,
as fishes arrive on the end of the stick.
As they arrive, they are placed in the basket,
the baskets made of reeds, that hold all the fish.
The freshly caught fish, will supply some food,
a meal for the family, upon which all of them depend,
depend on the fish, the fish from the lake,
which are cooked, which are grilled on the embers,
the hot embers, the embers of the fire still hot,
still hot, with the stones around still hot.
Fish cooked over the fire, with the fish well suspended,
suspended, pierced through by a stick.
They sizzle and crackle, with the flames from the fire,
the fire kept burning, for gathering, gatherings later.
For sitting around later, with the warmth of the fire,
for stories to be told, stories from long past,
past stories from history, tales of the Sioux.
The proud nation, who lived north on the plains.
We sit by the lake, and watch the reflections,
by the cool waters, under the wonderful sky.
The land of the free, but free no more.
We have our memories, and are now being retold.
Retelling the legends, the stories of old,
recite them by the lake, the lake with cool water,
the lake reflects history, history yet to be retold.

Image copyright Kate Roberts

Night time

In the dim water below, the fish are swimming around,
swimming around in the pale moonlight.
In the starlight from above the animals are around,
generally asleep, but occasionally one is abroad.
It is the wolf, padding around, seeing what is abroad,
sniffing around, treading carefully, carefully,
through the bushes and trees. The world seems asleep.
The world is silent, silent, except for the echoes,
the echoes of birds, of owls flying carefully above
looking for mice, for mice and small creatures,
to swoop down and grab, grab some food for themselves.
They land in a tree and perch on a branch, and by
the light from the moon will gobble their prey,
the skin and the bones, the body and all, then
swoop up again into the sky, and hunt for some more,
some more small animals, the voles and the mice,
any small creatures, swoops down in a trice,
and gather it up in claws that are sharp,
talons that are ready to swoop down on the prey,
the mice and the voles that scamper in the moonlight,
scamper in the moonlight, on their cycle of life,
about their business of gathering food for their families.
The fox, he wanders, he wanders and listens,
listens also for small animals wandering about.
The moon, it lights up the bushes and trees,
illuminating the world with the shafts of light,
creating the shadows with the moonbeams,
creating dark, secret places where animals may hide,
hide and escape from the wolf and the owl
and various animals walking stealthily around.

The morning sun rises up in the sky,
it gradually arrives with its wonderful hues,
the brilliant colours of the early morning sun,
the glorious glow as it rises over the horizon,
as slowly, slowly, the red glow appears, as it meets
the dark, dark blue sky up above,
gradually it rises up and up sparkling in the distance,
the wonderful purple red hue, then gradually red,
then the sun, magnificent, rises up in the sky.
The morning is fresh, with a gentle breeze.
The world that was so still, that appeared to be still,
except for the wolf, the fox and the owl,
not forgetting the small creatures that scampered below,
scampered in the moonlight, the shafts of moonlight,
now gone with the rise of the majestic sun,
the sun that warms all, all creatures from the chill
of the night time, lit only by the moon and the stars,
the stars up above, invisible for the moment, to return
with the moon, when the sun has crossed over the sky,
until the end of the day, another day,
in the rhythm of the seasons, the cycle of life.

The bird glides down

The bird glides low on the misty morning,
the bird flies down, to greet the world.
Nothing is stirring, it is the edge of morning,
sunrise, the brilliant sunrise, the start of a new day.
The bird, he appears, so pristine, so pristine,
glistening plumage of various hues.
The long tail feathers bob around as he balances.
He pauses a moment. The dewdrops are around,
hanging, suspended on various cobwebs,
glistening like jewels, jewels in the morning.
The gentle bird lands, so gently, so delicately,
so gently he settles with no one noticing,
so delicately he balances, on the branch of a tree.
So quietly he sits there with his beautiful plumage,
the tail feathers balancing, just keeping him steady.
The beautiful browns and russets for plumage,
a perfect creation, never copied by man.
The soft feathers of the plumage, underneath so soft.
The neat wing feathers in various hues,
this bird, perhaps, one would think of as 'dull',
no spectacular hues, no vivid colours!
But wait! Just look, just gaze, just study!
This bird is perfect! Complete! Just look!
There are various colours, if you just sit and look,
see him in flight, soar up into the sky.
The wings spread out, the wings interlacing,
he weaves and soars, hangs in the air currents,
he just hangs there and glides, glides on the wind,
the gentle wind of the early morning,
the early morning which heralds the sunrise.
The beginning of a new day, with the dewdrops hanging.
Our beautiful bird glides down with it's wings outstretched,
it slowly, softly comes down to land, tucking it's wings
to streamline it's body, with the tail balancing,
balancing the approach as it comes down to land,
to softly land on the branch of a tree,
where the dewdrops are hanging, in the early morning,
so gently, so gently he lands, that none of them judder!
The beautiful bird, a perfect creation!

THE BIRD FLIES DOWN TO GREET THE WORLD

Image copyright Kate Roberts

Footprints in the snow

Footprints in the snow, glistening in the snow,
in the moonlight, as it illuminates the world,
the silent world. The light from the moon above
directs its beams of light onto the earth below.
The earth, covered in varying depths,
where the snow has fallen and blown into crevices,
into cracks and secret places in the base of the hills,
the hills of North Dakota, the hills beside the plains.
The hills, when the snow falls and drifts down,
down, down, down, until it settles on the ground.
Then the winds come and whip up the snow,
whip it up, swirl it around, driving it down, down
into the base of the hills, near the plains.
The wind roars, roars in the moonlight,
roars across the snow and the ice,
roars with stinging, stinging cold.
Cold that freezes the breath, freezes the breath,
freezes the faces and hands of man.
But man turns away, with his back to the wind.
The time of moonlight is the time of sleep.
Days are short as the sun is low in the sky,
low in the sky at the beginning of day,
at the dawn of day, with it's pale yellow light
with no warmth, soon to sink in the sky.
When the moon appears with the stars
often obscured by grey and reddish clouds

scurrying across the sky, blown by
the wind in the clouds.
The clouds carrying snow and more snow,
more snow to fall on the hills and the valleys,
hiding the land and the trees, the trees to their tops,
the tops of the bare branches heavy with snow.
Icicles tinkle in the wind, in the gentle wind,
but if the wind roars, roars and rips through the trees,
the icicles are torn from the branches,
torn from the branches, blown away to be lost,
to be lost in the snowdrifts, created by the wind.
When the earth is still, with no snow falling,
nor wind roaring, over all the land,
the land is silent, the world is quiet, so quiet.
Peace at last from the falling snow and winds.
Peace, quiet to venture out and view the silent world,
the magic shapes made by nature and the reflection
of the moonlight in footprints in the snow,
to be lost in the snowdrifts created by the wind.
When the earth is still, with no snow falling,
nor wind roaring, over all of the land,
the land is silent, the world is quiet, so quiet.
Peace at last from the falling snow and winds.
Peace, quiet to venture out and view the silent world,
the magic shapes made by nature and the reflection
of the moonlight in footprints in the snow.

Springtime

The morning sun rises over the horizon.
Another morning begins, another day starts.
Another day for forgiving, another day for reflection.
The bees buzz around in the early sun.
Another warm day, a day of spring,
of the sun warming the earth after the winter cold.
The bees spread their wings in the warm sun,
buzzing and flying around on their quest,
their quest for nectar down in the flowers.
The bright flowers and blossoms nodding their heads
in the gentle warm breeze of the springtime.
The fields and hedges of the springtime,
full of flowers and blossoms, insects and birds.
Birds building their nests for laying their eggs,
the new season's clutch of eggs laid in the nests,
lying warm and protected by the birds that have them,
and continue to watch and protect them
from predators and foes that would enjoy the eggs,
who will steal the eggs, eggs for a meal.
But all of the eggs, hidden in the nests
are birds for the future, the next generation.
The parents protect the eggs in the nests,
so carefully constructed, so carefully placed
in the fork in the hedge or branch of a tree.
Eggs so carefully tended, so gently turned,

kept warm by the parent as the other one searches,
searches for food, for insects and water,
insects that fly in and out of the trees.
The eggs eventually will finally be ready,
ready to hatch, as cracks will appear, will appear
and spread over and around the shell.
The cracks will widen, and a beak will appear,
all wet and yellow, and slippery and slimey,
then more will appear, will follow the beak,
with feathers and body and an enormous cheep!
The chicks will emerge and wriggle and struggle,
to tumble over its mates, it's brothers and sisters.
Mum bird looks on and shakes them around!
The chicks will shake off the shell,
will clean their feathers for food,
then blink in the sunlight, the spring sunshine.
Then with a cheep, will hope for some insects,
fetched by the parents, in endless procession!
All mouths to be fed, with enormous wide beaks.
Parents hard at work, catching the insects,
the insects that roam around in the warm spring sun.
The time for new insects, new birds, new flowers,
and the birds and the bees that fly around
in the warmth of the spring sun.

Summertime

The grass in the meadows is full of
flowers, a spectrum of colour,
all the hues of the rainbow and all shades in between,
the blues and the purples, the pinks and the violets.
Short ones and tall, large ones and small,
fat ones and thin, together all the
creation of the WISE ONE,
the WISE ONE who created all,
for all mankind to see,
to see and enjoy, to see and to wonder,
the wonder of nature, not created by man.
To walk through the meadow, to see all the splendour,
the spectrum of colours not tainted by man.
The fulfilment of the seasons, the cycle of nature.
The height of the summer with the warm sunshine,
the brilliant sunshine after the rains of the spring,
the warmth of the summer sun
when everything flourishes.
The birds sing on high, sing in the hedgerows,
basking briefly in the sunshine,
pausing on their journey,
flying backwards and forwards,
finding food for their families,
busy, so busy with catching the
insects, diving for insects
that swarm over the meadows, insects
that hover and dart all around,
insects from hedgerows that hatch and emerge,
gather water from the dewdrops,
dewdrops in the hedgerow,
together with dewdrops in the flowers and the leaves.
When the soft summer rain falls, falls gently down,

down onto all life, especially on
the meadows and hedges,
in upturned petals and flowers
with their faces to the sun,
open and brilliant in the summer
day, but as the day cools
and the temperature drops, the bright sunshine dims
as the day wears on. Slowly, slowly the daylight fades,
and the evening coolness spreads over the land.
It heralds the evening, the end of the day.
The evening for gathering, the warmth needed
as everyone gathers around the evening fire.
The fire for cooking the evening meal
with the day's catch, be it fish or fowl,
or animal that was hunted
and killed for the pot, for the meal of the day,
as everyone gathers, gathers around the fire,
the fire that's for cooking, for warmth
and for comfort, comfort for everyone.
After the meal the telling
of stories, tales of long ago, long back
in history! Plans for the future,
talk of the family, the children and their
future, not knowing their future, their future
as planned would all come to nothing,
as history will tell, as man and his guns and
his greed for our land would soon be arriving
and drive us all out! Drive us all out,
away from the land, the land of our fathers,
the land with our futures, the land with the
meadows with the beautiful flowers.

The soft summer rain

The soft summer rain falls, gently, gently, gently.
It trickles down silently, so different from the winter snow.
A different world, but we live here, we are used to it.
We are used to the wide open spaces, space to move,
to move with the seasons, as the grass grows.
We are many, we need the space for animals.
Cattle we move as the grass is eaten, is cropped short.
We move them to find new pastures, new grass for our animals.
We meet other Sioux in our travels, others to talk to,
to exchange news of the wide, the wide open spaces,
spaces the WISE ONE provided for all, for all people.
The pastures, the rocks and the mountains, streams and the rivers,
water for us and for our animals, for washing and drinking.
The cool water, still cool in the summer, but pure water,
organised by the WISE ONE, so well planned!
Provided for all, for us all to share in the bounty,
the bounty of the earth, to be shared by all mankind.
An uncomplicated life, the way life should be for us all,
until man with his guns arrived! Arrived, to move us all,
to chase us away, to take all our land, the land where we lived!
They did not care, they took our land, chased us away,
killed us with their guns, chased us away!
Cruel men, intent on the land for themselves!
But there was plenty of land, but they would not share!
We defended our land the WISE ONE had given, given to all men,
but man has changed! Men with their guns and their weapons to kill,
just raided our lands and chased us away, away to be lost,
or so the men thought, the men with their guns,
but we could not be 'lost,' some of us lived, we could escape!
Just a few of us lived, those who escaped with our lives!
Most of the young men, the men who were 'braves',
they fought and they fought! They knew the land, the hills
and the valleys, the plateaus and crevices!
Their horses were fast, their arrows were good, but man and his guns,
they chased us away! They shot with their guns, again and again! Some children escaped,
and women with child, but most of the braves, they fought to the end!
The men with the guns, some of them stayed,
stayed on the land the WISE ONE had given, had given to us all!
Now the land, it has changed, but the soft gentle rain,
the gentle rain, the rain of summer has not changed,
it is part of the seasons in the land of our fathers.

Smoke rises from the fire

Smoke rises from fire, the evening fire where everyone is gathered
for the end of the day. The smoke curls up and up, spiralling
into the heavens, spiralling, twisting and turning, curling around,
curling around, up, up into the sky. The beautiful azure sky,
the clear blue sky, the clear blue sky of North Dakota,
land of the Sioux, the Sioux people, the ancient people,
descended, descended from people from a far- off land.
We came across the snows, to cross in the winter,
to cross in the winter, when the sea was frozen, many moons ago!
We are a proud people, a proud people with many traditions.
We keep these traditions with our story telling. Stories that are true,
all so true. We tell our tales as we sit around the evening fire.
Sometimes we just sit and meditate, follow our own thoughts.
The Wise ones speak, never the younger ones.
The Wise ones will bring a thought and develop it.
Then the Wise one will talk, after many thoughts, many thoughts,
much meditation to bring to the gathering, maybe a thought
that is developing and bringing wisdom. No one speaks,
no one utters a word, until invited to speak.
The Wise one's thoughts are developing, asking for guidance,
for guidance from the WISE ONE above, the Wise One of all,
who created all at the beginning, created our nation
when we lived across the snows. We are able to reach the WISE ONE
if we meditate! This is where our wisdom comes from,
but it only comes to wise men who are patient, are patient and sit
and ponder, sit and meditate. This is the essence of life to sit and meditate,
to reach for the wisdom, the wisdom that is there.
To access wisdom one must have experience, experience of life,
to understand through life, to acknowledge the wisdom of the elders,
with wisdom for the young ones who must wait and respect,
to wait and be patient, to listen to the Wise ones. To learn, to listen,
to wait until they accept the wisdom, from father to son, from father to son,
over many moons. To gather around, as the evening shadows fall,
as the evening shadows grow longer and the air chills, even in summer
in North Dakota. As we all sit around the evening fire,
watching the smoke curl up from the fire and dream our dreams
and in dreaming our dreams we may reach the WISE ONE.

Copyright Kate Roberts

The cycle of the seasons.

The raindrops, as the summer rain, then later into the fall,
the fall when the hedgerows change, the colours change,
the beautiful colours of the fall, when the days are shorter.
The reds and the browns, the yellows from the green,
the green leaves from the summer time, to change,
to change to all the russet colours, the colours of the fall,
the time of nuts and berries, the fruits of the hedgerow.
Foods for everyone and the nuts to keep for the winter,
the winter when food is short and the weather is colder.
Nuts and berries for the birds, nuts and berries
that drop down to the ground, down, down to the ground
to where small animals scamper and find the berries,
the nuts and berries that fall and roll into the roots.
The mists of the fall, the time of stillness,
the time when cobwebs appear, covered in dew.
Gaze, my child, gaze into the interior, pause and look.
Look, stay awhile, see the world beyond,
the world to be seen, if you stand and look.
Stand and wonder at the beautiful threads, the beautiful patterns,
woven so deftly by the spider, the delicate spider.
Each spider is working and weaving, working and weaving,
in and out, backwards and forwards, backwards and forwards.
Gaze, my child, at this wonder of nature, so magnificent,
a wonder to behold, created so deftly, created so carefully.
Such patience, my child, such absolute patience,
and dedication to the task in hand, woven and woven,
in and out, up and down, intricate patterns,
woven and woven until the task is complete!
Do we finish, do we complete such tasks to the end?
To persevere, to continue, to keep on and on,
as the spider, as he weaves, weaves his cobweb!
A task of perfection, so perfect, completed, shown in the dew,
in the dew of the morning, shining in the sunlight,
amongst the leaves of the fall, the russets and browns, yellows and reds.
All waiting my child, for us to gaze and wonder.
The wonder of nature created by the WISE ONE.
Stop my child, stop and gaze at the wonder of nature,
the leaves of the fall, as the world changes, in the cycle of nature.

The sun is lower

The sun is lower, at the turn of the seasons, the time of change,
the change of the leaves, the colour of the world.
The air is cooler, the fire is needed to warm us all,
needed for comfort and also for light, but especially the warmth.
The glow of the embers, the sparkle of the flames as they dance,
as they dance and rise up and dance with various colours,
rise up into the sky. The smoke curls up and up, up into the stars,
taking our thoughts, taking our thoughts as we gaze
and watch the smoke drift up and up into the stars.
A time for reflection and meditation, time for quiet and thought,
watching the smoke curl up and up, up into the stars,
taking our thoughts with it. A special time, a time to escape,
a time apart, with just our thoughts, and away from reality.
Daydreams, but guided daydreams, time to dwell on life,
life and its meaning, the meaning of life. Life, and where
we are going and why we are here? Plans for the future,
for our families and friends. But, where are we going?
We did not know that other men, other men from another world
would arrive with their guns, their guns and their greed,
would chase us all out, away from our world, our dreams and our hopes,
our land, given by the WISE ONE! The WISE ONE had other plans,
other plans for our destiny, but we will survive, we will survive
down through history, but life, not as we knew it, life that we had
in our land given by the WISE ONE! No! So different! So different
from our plans for the future, the plans that we had as we sat
around our fire, as we gathered around the fire, the fire of the evening,
as we sat and watched the smoke, the smoke from the fire, as it curled up
and up, up and up with our dreams, with our dreams for the future.
As the sun lowers, lowers in the sky, as the days are shorter,
we light our fire, the wood and the sparks, the sparks shoot like fairies,
fairies of the spirit! The embers, they glow, glow various colours,
colours of the leaves, the leaves of the trees, the leaves
as they change colour in the cool of the season. Similar colours,
beautiful colours to dress up the trees, the trees of the fall,
before the snows come. But for now, the embers of the fire
remind us of the colours, the beautiful colours.
The sun sinks lower in the sky, the beginning of winter.

The perfume of the world

Each person is alive, is aware of the smells and the senses,
the perfumes of the world, of the world. Breezes, gentle breezes,
which bring the scent of flowers, the beautiful scent of flowers,
the pollen and the petals, the gentle flow of the perfume,
especially in the morning, the early morning, when the sun
has just risen, just risen from the stars. The earth is wet,
is wet with the early morning dew! Time when the cobwebs
appear, appear in their beautiful forms, as you wander
in the early morning when the sun is rising and bringing warmth
to the world, when the cobwebs are brilliant and the flowers
are awakening, awakening and nodding their heads towards
the early sun, the early sun and it's warming rays.
The flowers nod their heads and the perfume from the flowers,
almost invisible, wafts on the breeze, the gentle breeze,
bringing the perfume, the delicate perfume, for man to catch,
if he is early enough! Early morning is when the senses
are heightened, before the tasks of the day, the day
is a distraction. To wander and look, to pause and breathe in,
breathe in the early morning air, the cool air, with the sun
just rising from the stars, with the warmth of the sun,
when the air is fresh and cool with the early morning mist.
The time to pause and look. Pause awhile and smell the air,
the perfume of the flowers, nodding and rising in the early morning.
To see the cobwebs, watch the spiders completing their task,
and the smell of the damp earth, newly damp from the early
morning dew. The world is waking up, all is quiet.
Time for reflection, time to pause, to tarry awhile,
pause to inhale the perfume of the flowers in the early morning.

The water trickles down

The water trickles gently over the stones, the cold water of the early fall.
The water is still cold, although the snows on the hills have long melted.
The water coming from the springs in the hills is still cold,
so very cold, despite running and rattling over the stones,
the stones and pebbles that lie at the bottom of the stream,
despite the summer sun and now the late summer sun,
as the nights become earlier and the sun becomes weaker,
the summer sun has not warmed the clear water, the spring water,
the water from the hills, the pure water, the blue water.
It chuckles along, chuckling and bubbling between the boulders
and stones, boulders and stones, both large and both small,
creating a path, creating a highway for the water, a path
twisting and turning, twisting and turning, this way and that,
sharp corners and bends, sudden twists and turns, and then
drops down, where water chuckles and tinkles
and tumbles over the stones, splashing and splashing,
sending spray in the air, creating rainbows when the sun shines!
Creating rainbows of beautiful colours, creating rainbows
where fairies gather, gather in the spray and the beautiful colours,
gather in the joy of living. The joy of the sunshine, the spray,
and the colours, the colours of the rainbow! Peace! Peace
near the tinkling water. Peace, peace, quiet and magic. Just special,
so special, peace, where there is magic! No man to interfere!
Peace, just peace! A privilege to visit, to find, to stay,
to be wrapped in the atmosphere, nature, as the WISE ONE created,
a special place, untouched by man! Innocence, innocence
by the cool waters, the tinkling water, as it tumbles over the rocks
and stones, sending spray into the air, into the air, for the sun's rays
to glow through the water and show the world the beautiful colours
of the rainbow, as the water showers down, down onto the green plants
and herbs around, and down into the stream, the stream
as it continues on its way, on its journey, the endless journey,
on and on, through the fields and the woods, on its endless journey,
always cold, always clear, rattling over the stones, the water
which comes from the springs in the hills in North Dakota,
endless, timeless, never failing, always clear, beautiful spring water.

Ferns and their mysteries

The ferns in the grass are growing well,
hidden under the trees and shady corners,
hidden well, the dark colours, the dark green of the fronds,
the fronds with the brown seeds hidden behind.
The fern's leaves with serrated edges, the split edges,
the edges quite sharp if you run your fingers down
and along the edges. The fern's dark green shades,
brown underneath, with hidden seeds, a wonderful aroma,
even when crushed! A quiet, hidden world. Peaceful!
Peaceful, an escape! To sit quietly, to absorb oneself
in the green colour, to surround oneself with the vivid
colour of life itself, to sit and meditate within. Surrounded
and enveloped within the colour of life, to renew and recharge.
Ferns have many stories to tell as they have come from ancient
times immemorial, of ancient times, memories of life long ago,
as life started, the dawn of time, created by the WISE ONE.
Secret tales as life passed around them, of ancient man,
of early man, early innocence. History of man, man came and went,
backwards and forwards, forwards in time, but unrecorded,
unrecorded in history for man to remember, only surmise,
with various clues. But the plants of the ancients hold many secrets,
of life that passed around them, of past generations.
Sit amongst a bed of ferns. Sit and hold a leaf,
run your finger over a leaf, and sense the mysteries!

Copyright Kate Roberts

Winter

The snow is high and the wind is
blowing, blowing, blowing!
It comes in gusts around the tepees,
shakes the walls and
buffets the flaps, the flap at the entrance, tied down,
still lifts the edges, allowing the
wind in through the gaps,
the gaps around the flaps. Winter is
here, the time of the snows,
the time of short days, short days and long nights.
Short days of little daylight. So cold,
so cold, but warm in the tepees.
We have skins on the floors, to keep
us warm from the cold,
the cold on the ground. We have skins
to sit on and skins as a cloak.
We have time to talk, to talk over the
long days, the long warm days,
and days long past, the tales of our
people. History you would call it!
Winter is cold and we are hungry.
We have to go hunting.
The men and young braves, we go
hunting, hunting with our arrows.
It is hard work to keep moving, keep
moving through the snow.
We move cautiously, we move carefully,
move carefully through the snow.
We use bushes and tree trunks,
using them for camouflage.
We hope to draw nearer an animal we
see. We set up a plan, a plan
which involves different groups approaching the prey.
We move in slowly, silently, downwind of the animal.
We have a plan and signals we use, moving our arms
to signal and communicate. We must remain silent!
When we are near enough we use our
arrows, hopefully accurate!
But, not always accurate! Our hands
are cold. But if we miss,

perhaps the other group will
manage as it runs their way!
All the time we are teaching the young boys as well,
passing our skills on, from time
immemorial. Times long past,
wisdom passed on through many, many generations.
If we should succeed, the kill is
collected and carried or dragged
between us. We need all the carcass,
the skin and the bone.
All will be used, all will be used.
The meat will be eaten,
the carcass carefully stripped, roasted in
sections, cooked on the hot stones,
the hot stones around the fire, the
stones heated in the embers.
The meat is eagerly eaten as all will
be hungry, all will be hungry.
We are careful with our food store,
meat and fish caught
in the days of plenty, in the time of long
days, it will have been smoked,
smoked over the fire, suspended over
the fire, suspended in the smoke,
in the smoke from the fire. We add bracken
and herbs, bracken and herbs
to the wood on the fire, to produce an
evocative smell, special smoke
for the meat, special smoke for the
fish. This preserves the food,
extends the larder for the lean days,
the days of winter, the days
when we see no sun, the short
days and the long nights,
when the snow falls and the wind
blows in gusts, in gusts
around the tepees. The wind blows
and blows! The weather,
so cold, so cold in the short days, time
of the wind and the snow.

Watch the sunrise

The arc of the sun, the sun as it rises, as it rises up
over the edge of the world, from the world of night,
of the blue sky, the deep blue of the world of starlight.
We dream of this world, in the depth of winter, of the cold
and the snow. We dream of the sun rising in the early
morning, in the early morning. The blessed sun,
the sun of warmer days, of longer days! The sun, as it rises
with the beautiful arc of colours, of so many colours,
colours in nature around us, colours most beautiful.
Sit and dream, my friends, of the sunlight, as the sun rises.
The wonderful hues and shades of purples, then reds,
then pinks, then finally the sun bursts forth, bursts forth
into the sky, now pale orange, now slipping into yellow.
A splendid sight, the magic of the morning, as the sun rises.
The early morning the sun rises, the magnificent silence
at the start, the beginning, the beginning of a new day.
The colours of sunrise, so special, the amazing colours,
so many hues! The gift of the WISE ONE! So few people
realise this wonderful gift! The pure, pure colours
seen with each sunrise, the sunrise of the morning.
A gift for us all! Sit in the quiet, the quiet of the sunrise,
seen in the silence, the silence, absorbed by the inner eye.
To recall in the winter, the depths of winter, the short days
of the times of the snows, the cold and the winds, the gusty winds.
All are cold, and possibly hungry, but dream of the sunrise,
the beautiful sunrise, the rays of the sun and the springtime,
the springtime to come, the warmth of the sun's rays, all come to life.

The beginning of spring

The wind blows gently through the trees, the gentle breeze of spring,
time when the days become longer and the nights shorter,
time when the snow begins to melt on the lower slopes,
the lower slopes of the hills, and gradually, gradually the snows melt
and the edge of the snow retreats, retreats up the hills.
The melted snows cascade down the mountains and the hills,
to rush down gullies and slopes, down, down, down,
down into the valleys below. To bubble and gather, trickle
and trickle down into the streams below. So cold, so cold
from the winter snow melting and melting, to expose the hills
gradually higher and higher to slowly become covered
with the greens of spring growth. The sun will warm,
will warm the slopes, to allow the grass to grow once more,
eventually bathed in the spring sunshine, the gentle warmth,
as the sun rises higher and higher up in the sky.
The days become longer, and everything stirs again, with the joy
of spring! All have waited patiently for the skies to be clearer,
for the snow clouds to blow away, for this year at least.
For the sun to begin to peep through, the promise of the season to come,
the season of growth, growth of the grass, to provide for the
various animals. We move up with the meadows, for the animals to feed,
and for us to hunt, to hunt for the buffalo and other animals.
Food for us all, the women and children, women and children,
all who have been hungry through the lean winter, months and months
of the cold, of the cold and the snows. The cold of winter,
soon to be passed, soon to be a memory, a time now gone!
We look forward to the warmth of the sun, the cold just a memory,
just a memory! But beware, a warning, a reminder for prudence,
for prudence to look forward to the future of the next winter
snows, next winter snows, time of the short days. Plan for the
short days with preserving some meat, some fish and some game.
We will eat some, and keep some, some from every repast,
as stores will be needed for the next cold season,
the time of the snows, the time of the short days.
But for now we will bask in the sunshine, the warm days of spring,
the season of the sun's emergence and the soft warmer breezes of spring.

Summer flowers

The summer flowers arrive with the blessed
sun after the long days of the winter snows.
When spring arrives, with the
emergence of everything,
of all plants and animals, insects and bees.
The plants grow and the buds grow and fatten,
and eventually, after the spring rains
the buds open and become flowers,
flowers of various hues and colours of varying intensity,
of reds and pinks, yellows and blues,
of various shades and various hues,
to brighten the world and attract the insects,
especially the bees collecting the pollen.
Collecting the pollen from the base of the flowers,
inside the flowers at the base of the petals.
Some of the flowers, the vivid colours, the vivid hues,
the reds and the oranges, the pinks and the blues.

The vivid yellow flowers, especially the yellow,
are carefully gathered in their separate colours.
Each of the colours are gathered together,
the petals removed from the rest of the flower,
the petals are gathered and more of them gathered,
all put together in the hollow of a stone.
Another stone, which fits, is now used to grind them,
to grind them all up into a pulp.
All the bright colour stays in the hollow
and covered with leaves to keep it all cool.
It will then be used for adorning the bodies,
for special occasions when bodies are painted
with various designs and various symbols,
all vivid with stripes, with the yellow the best,
the various hues and various colours,
colours obtained from the wondrous summer flowers.

Copyright Kate Roberts

Why, Why Worry?

There are lots of things in life, lots of things, of blessings,
but remain true to the things you like,
gardens and avenues, sunshine and showers,
wonders of nature, the birds in the skies.
Apple blossom and pear, birds on the wing,
sunshine and showers, the best of everything.
Things that cost nothing comfort you in stress.
Do not worry, do not fret, my friend.
Just value what you have, the trees, the grass,
the blue sky up above. Many things, many things to bring you joy,
to bring you joy. Remember all the blessings, all the blessings
that you have, true joy, true happiness with what surrounds you.
You are YOU and only you who stands alone.
You are strong within yourself. You need nature around you,
with the trees and the flowers, the birds and the bees,
the birds in the sky. You have your own space, a space to think.
There is much to reflect on, much to explore.
Life is exciting, research never ending.
Just look around you, you will be surprised!
Open your eyes, open your ears.
You are never alone, never ever alone.
Keep your mind open, the world is before you.

Acknowledgements

A big thank you to my friend Ewa Thorley who has helped me through all the complexities of finally getting this ready for presenting to the publisher.

Also to my son, Ben Loryman, who has given me both his time and assistance. Thank you.

Printed in the United States
by Baker & Taylor Publisher Services